I LOVE ME I LOVE YOU 5

GUIDEBOOK

SPIRITUAL MEANINGS OF THE
CHARACTERS AND THEIR LIFE LESSONS
YOU ARE GUIDED SAFELY HOME

BY ANNE PRYOR, M.A.

Copyright ©2025 by Anne Pryor.

All rights reserved. This book or any portion thereof may not be reproduced or used in any manner whatsoever without the express written permission of the publisher except for the use of brief quotation in a book review. Thank you.

This guidebook holds a deep and tender story, one that begins with Anne's mother's own journey through fear, faith, and love at the end of her life.

Anne's mother lived with a heavy burden. From an early age, she was told by her religion that she was "dirty" and filled with original sin. This message made her believe she was unworthy, that she was flawed, and that she deserved punishment. The weight of this belief haunted her throughout her life, and especially as she faced the end, she was terribly afraid of dying. She feared being sent to "hell" and struggled to find peace.

During Anne's two-year care for her mother, it was a hard and painful time. Priests were called regularly for confession, hoping it would ease her fears and bring comfort. But even these rituals seemed to fall short of lifting the deep sadness and terror within. The journey was filled with heartbreak and uncertainty.

After her mother passed away, Anne began receiving messages that profoundly transformed her understanding of life and death. Her mother's soul communicated that at the moment of passing, each soul faces a choice: to follow the darkness or to move toward the light. Those messages became seeds of healing—not only for Anne's family, but for every child and adult who reads these stories.

That is why Anne wrote the I Love Me I Love You series, a gift born from love and truth. The stories in the five books share the beautiful teachings Anne's mother brought from the other side—messages that all children are perfect

just as they are, made from God's light and created in God's own image. They carry unconditional love in their hearts— "puffs of love" to share freely. They learn that speaking their truth, even when it is hard, brings healing both to themselves and to others, including souls who have hurt them or whom they have lost.

Most of all, Anne's mother shared that God wants every soul to come home, to the spirit world, heaven, filled with peace, love, and light. God wants no one left behind, no matter what. We each have guardian angels and divine spirit guides who journey with us, helping us safely return to heaven when we leave our human bodies. And we should never be afraid to ask God for help.

This book, I Love Me I Love You 5: You Are Guided Safely Home, invites children, and all readers, to travel with Devin and friends through moments of darkness and uncertainty, always finding the bright light that leads us safely back to God's loving embrace. It is a story of courage, hope, and the unbreakable truth that we are never alone.

May this guidebook be a loving companion on your own journey, a reminder that you are perfect, deeply loved, and always guided safely home.

Blessings on you,

Annie

Scout the Spaceship

SPIRITUAL MEANING:

Scout reminds us that we belong in the vast universe and that seeing life from a higher perspective brings peace and wonder. He symbolizes the cosmic light that shines within each of us, connecting us to the stars and to the feeling of home, no matter where we travel.

LIFE LESSON:

Be curious and playful. Your inner light is bright and guiding trust that you are always safely guided toward your true home.

AUTHOR'S NOTE:

Scout encourages us to shine our unique light, appreciate the journeys of others, and remember that even in darkness, music and friendship can light the way.

REFLECTIVE QUESTIONS:

1. When you consider your own life's journey, how does shifting to a broader, universal perspective change your feelings about death or the unknown?

2. Can you recognize the "inner light" that guides you even when fear arises? How might embracing that light ease your worry about dying?

3. How might viewing death as a "safe return home" transform your grief or anxiety about loss?

Eureka Escalator

SPIRITUAL MEANING:

Eureka symbolizes the journey between worlds—the uplifting transition from worry to hope, from uncertainty to faith. She represents the bridges we cross with trust, connecting earth and heaven, and guiding each step safely.

LIFE LESSON:

Trust the journey. Heaven is loving, welcoming, and always open to you. Let your heart climb toward the light with courage and grace.

AUTHOR'S NOTE:

Eureka's shimmering rainbows remind us that in moments of worry we can call on faith and find our footing again. When Anne's mother came back to her, she said that she had a choice, to go with the dark entities that she saw or go with her husband, who had passed, to the light.

After much consternation, Anne's mother chose to go with her husband to the light, like superman and superwoman, according to her mom's messages. Now, Anne's mother is enjoying time with God, family and friends, is healing, learning, and sharing messages with Anne from the spirit-side. She's so happy now.

REFLECTIVE QUESTIONS:

1. How do you personally experience the "bridges" or transitions between life and whatever lies beyond?

2. What role does trust play in your understanding of death and what comes after?

3. How can embracing the idea of heaven as a loving, welcoming place help you confront fears of the unknown?

Kiki Kite

SPIRITUAL MEANING:

Kiki is the spirit of freedom, boldness, and courage in the face of uncertainty. She shows that storms are part of growth, and that navigating winds with trust reveals new beauty and strength.

LIFE LESSON:

Trust the wind, even when it blows wild. Storms bring change and growth, and with courage, you will always find your way through.

AUTHOR'S NOTE:

Kiki teaches that it's okay to feel scared sometimes, and that friends and imagination can lift us through the toughest winds to safety. Anne's mom was tangled in her own thoughts that she couldn't get rid of. Bad thoughts, her mom used to say. In after-death messages, Anne's mom said that she wished that she would have asked for and received more mental health help.

REFLECTIVE QUESTIONS:

1. What "storms" in your life have shaped your understanding of mortality and the impermanence of being?

2. How do you cope with fear when life feels uncertain, especially regarding the end of life?

3. In what ways can you cultivate courage to "trust the wind" when facing death or grief?

Benu Bird

SPIRITUAL MEANING:

Benu Bird embodies renewal, spiritual guidance, and the radiant connection to the sun and cycles of rebirth. Her joyful song calls forth spiritual helpers and light, symbolizing the promises of new beginnings and faithful support.

LIFE LESSON:

With loving support and joyful encouragement, trying new things helps you find unexpected strength and discover your true path home.

AUTHOR'S NOTE:

Benu's songs remind us that we are never alone; even when skies darken, the faith and music of friendship will always lift us safely.

REFLECTIVE QUESTIONS:

1. How do the themes of rebirth and renewal resonate with your beliefs about life after death?

2. Who or what are the "spiritual helpers" in your life that offer strength when you face fears about mortality?

3. How might embracing a sense of joyful renewal help you transform grief or fear around dying?

Azeria Angel

SPIRITUAL MEANING:

Azeria Angel represents spiritual guidance, honoring the Earth, and the deep connectedness of all living beings. She reflects the nurturing spirit within us those cares for the planet and stands guard beside us with unseen friends.

LIFE LESSON:

We are caretakers of Gaia, supported by spirit friends and guardian angels who walk with us always, guiding us safely home through kindness and love.

AUTHOR'S NOTE:

Azeria's presence reminds us of the power of kindness, the strength of community, and the comfort that comes from knowing we are never alone. Anne's mom shared that she had received a "puff of love" in her heart before she passed. Anne believes that Angel Ezekiel worked with God to replace her heart of stone with a heart of love.

Anne prays to her guardian angel, whom she has named Azeriah, to help her and her mom to heal. Anne places an open chair in each of her rooms to allow her guardian angel to sit with her during the day, and at night when she sleeps.

REFLECTIVE QUESTIONS:

1. How does the idea of guardian angels and spiritual guides impact your view of death as a passage rather than an ending? What name would you give your guardian angel?

2. What practices or beliefs help you feel connected to the Earth and to your "spirit family" in times of loss or fear?

3. How can cultivating kindness toward yourself and others deepen your trust in the loving guidance that surrounds you?

SUMMARY TABLE FOR FACILITATORS, TEACHERS, AND THERAPISTS

Character	Spiritual Meaning	Life Lesson
Scout the Spaceship	Feeling at home in the universe; seeing the world's beauty from above.	Be curious, playful, and know you are always guided.
Eureka Escalator	Upliftment, transition between worlds.	Trusting the journey—Heaven is loving and welcoming.
Kiki Kite	Freedom, courage through uncertainty.	Trusting the wind; storms bring growth and beauty.
Benu Bird	Renewal, spiritual guidance, connection to the sun and rebirth.	With loving support, trying new things helps you find strength for your journey.
Azeria Angel	Spiritual guidance, honoring the Earth, connectedness.	We are each caretakers of Gaia, with spirit friends always near.

Final Reflection
The Power of 5A's

As you support children and adults in exploring these adventures and spiritual lessons, encourage them to practice the 5A's:

Ask for guidance and help from God, Jesus, angels, divine and sacred spirit guides, and friends, when feeling lost or afraid.

Allow yourself to receive the messages that you hear and comfort and support from friends, angels, and spirit guides.

Accept the messages as they are, and feel the presence of love and healing, even if it feels subtle or different than expected.

Appreciate and be grateful, give thanks for all the moments of kindness, courage, and connection as signs of being truly supported; and finally,

Anne Pryor, M.A., is a children's book author and the creator of Lovitude™, and a Soul Painter. This art form fuses love and gratitude-energies she believes are the highest in the universe. Her vibrant artwork has been featured worldwide, including at the Mayo Clinic, and is licensed on products distributed globally.

Anne's journey as an artist began unexpectedly after she received profound after-death communications from her late mother and a close friend. These spiritual encounters inspired her to create soul paintings and, more recently, to write a children's book. Her stories are rooted in the message she received from her mother: that every child is born perfect, without original sin-a message of inherent goodness and divine connection to God that she now shares.

Before embracing her calling as a Soul Painter and author, Anne was a successful corporate executive, holding marketing leadership roles and as the first employee to open Mall of America's Knott's Camp Snoopy, where she collaborated with Charles Schulz (who is one of her Spirit Guides), and his team. Drawing on her business acumen, Anne became a renowned LinkedIn strategist and executive coach, helping leaders and organizations cultivate authentic connections and meaningful online presence.

Anne holds a Master's Degree in Human Development, and her philosophy of interconnectedness and purpose infuses both her art and her coaching. She is a sought-after speaker, recognized for her work in authentic leadership, heart-centered business, and the transformative power of love and gratitude.

Residing in Minnesota, Anne continues to inspire through her Lovitude Soul Paintings, keynote presentations, and children's books. She invites everyone to remember their soul's purpose, embrace their innate goodness, and recognize that we are all connected, here to do our highest good. Connect with Anne Pryor on LinkedIn or visit www.Lovitude.com to explore her art, books, and insights.